July, 2014

Marlowe—
You have spent
much time nurturing
the residents at 928... now
remember to take time for you!

Sheila, Kath, Edith
Packer, Busby i Barley

PAUSITIVITY

noun: The feeling of joy and optimism that comes when you stop to take a moment to restore and nurture yourself.

...BALANCE IS THE AIM OF ALL LIVING
CREATURES; IT IS OUR HOME.

Rolf Gates

Leave room in every day for calm and joy to grow.

SOMETIMES THE MOST IMPORTANT
THING IN A WHOLE DAY IS THE REST WE
TAKE BETWEEN TWO DEEP BREATHS...

Etty Hillesum

Close your eyes. Breathe deeply.
Notice the sounds of the world around you.

WHEN YOU RECOVER OR DISCOVER
SOMETHING THAT NOURISHES
YOUR SOUL AND BRINGS JOY, CARE
ENOUGH ABOUT YOURSELF TO
MAKE ROOM FOR IT IN YOUR LIFE.

Jean Shinoda Bolen

*Tend a garden, call a friend, re-read a book
you've always loved. Cultivate happiness.*

THIS IS A BEAUTIFUL AND SIMPLE CHANGE
OF LIFESTYLE. A LIFESTYLE OF LETTING
GO AND LIVING OPENHANDEDLY, CURLED
UP IN THE SUNLIT WARMTH...

Julie Sarah Powell

Soak in the sunlight, savor simple contentment.

ONE OF THE BEST THINGS
YOU CAN DO WHEN THE
WORLD IS STORMING
AROUND YOU IS TO PAUSE.

Mitch Thrower

Find stillness at the center of the storm.
Keep your mind calm and your heart warm.

TENSION IS WHO YOU THINK YOU
SHOULD BE. RELAXATION IS WHO YOU ARE.
Chinese Proverb

Cherish saying yes to the things that matter most.

SMILE, BREATHE AND GO SLOWLY.

Thich Nhat Hanh

Be still for a moment. The world will wait.

DON'T LET YOUR MIND BULLY YOUR BODY INTO
BELIEVING IT MUST CARRY THE BURDEN OF ITS WORRIES.

Astrid Alauda

Quiet yourself. Rest your body. Open your heart.

WHEN OUR MIND IS QUIET,
WHEN OUR MIND IS IN SILENCE,
THEN THE NEW ARRIVES.

Samael Aun Weor

Lean into the unknown with faith.
Make room for new miracles.

...BE SILENT...AND THE BEAUTY EXPLODES, REACHES TO YOU FROM ALL DIRECTIONS. YOU ARE DROWNED IN THE BEAUTY OF A SUNRISE, OF A STARRY NIGHT, OF BEAUTIFUL TREES.

Osho

Rest your back against a tree. Take in the sky.
Count the birds. Find peace, and carry it with you.

HOW BEAUTIFUL IT IS TO DO NOTHING,
AND THEN TO REST AFTERWARD.

Spanish Proverb

Today, your simply being is enough.

LAUGHTER RELAXES.
AND RELAXATION IS SPIRITUAL.

Bhagwan Shree Rajneesh

Laugh, and let your light shine through.